Garden G

D0286525

A No Nonsense, No PhD Guide to Great Gardens

With Hand-Holding How To's for Beginners

And Straightforward Instruction for Advanced Gardeners

Written By:

Sarah Olver

Entire contents protected by U.S. copyright, 2013

Dedication

To my husband, Jeff, my sons, Nathan and Corton, and the Creator of the very first garden. My life is a garden because of you all.

Contents

Introduction

My garden is my most beautiful masterpiece. ~
Claude Monet

A single slip of clean paper, twenty or so sleeves of seeds, a sketching pencil, and one very large, very empty backyard garden--thus began my gardening career fifteen years ago. Young, naïve, and cash poor from having just purchased our first home, our landscaping budget combined with a lack of horticultural experience equaled the perfect storm. I read every package of seeds, front and back. I made copious notes about their potential heights, their colors, and the time of year they would each bloom. This garden, I was determined, would be the envy of all my retired-nothing-better-to-do-than-fiddle-in-their-gardens-senior-citizen-neighbors.

With the greatest care I had selected larkspur, purple coneflower, phlox, lupines, shasta daisies, and a passel of other flowers. I dug little trenches in which to plant my precious seeds and tenderly tucked each of them into the earth. Lightly covering the bed that stretched the entire width of my backyard with soil, I finished my project just before a late evening storm rolled over the flat land of Southern Ontario. Pleased, I sipped iced tea as I watched the rain bathe my seeds. Then patiently, day after day, I began what would become a lifelong spring-time ritual. Coffee in hand, I walked the garden perimeter every single morning and afternoon sleuthfully checking for any signal of life--a sprig of green, a sliver or shoot sprouting up from the earth.

Naturally, the senior neighbors dropped in during the process. Proudly, I showed them my sketch describing in great detail just how perfect the garden would be. They remained prim and strangely silent. And faithfully, I walked the perimeters, waiting and hoping.

Eventually green shoots did indeed begin to sprout--thousands upon thousands of them. And they all appeared so similar. I congratulated myself on my excellent soil and told myself all plants must resemble one another in the early stages. What I had done had saved us countless dollars and would soon be a backyard fit for small bridal parties. I actually volunteered my garden for such an occasion informing the bride that there would most definitely be flowers by her big day. I was certain.

Certainly mistaken.

The green shoots? Weeds. All of them.

It took several months and not a few subtle hints from my sweet senior neighbors before I finally accepted defeat and bought a few sparse plants to spread across my precious weed garden. That my first masterpiece was a dismal failure is no small understatement. Perhaps though, that isn't entirely true. It was there, as the grains of sweet Ontario soil slinked through my fingers, that I fell in love with what happens when dirt and root, sun and rain, and human hands come together to paint a mural on an earthen canvas.

If, like me, you are about to embark on your first foray into the foreign arena of gardening, you are in good company. "A new study from local market research firm Scarborough reveals that of the nearly 164 million homeowners in the United States, nearly half (49 percent) gardened in the past 12 months." ("Nearly Half of All American Homeowners Give a Green Thumbs-Up to Home Improvements") Frankly, it is about time you joined the party. Not only is outdoor landscape good for the environment, it happens to offer a lot of bang for your investment buck too. "A well maintained landscape with mature trees can increase property values up to 25 percent. Trees can cool houses in the summer. A city lot with 30 percent plant cover provides the equivalent cooling necessary to air condition two moderately sized houses 12 hours a day in the summer." ("Talking Trees An Urban Forestry Toolkit for Local Governments")

In his book, *The Education of a Gardener,* Russell Page said, "If you wish to make anything grow, you must understand it, and understand it in a very real sense. 'Green fingers' are a fact, and a mystery only to the unpracticed. But green fingers are the extensions of a verdant heart." (Page)

Ultimately, gardening is no more difficult than frying an egg or tossing a salad. With a bit of instruction, a bit of earth and root, and a "verdant heart" anyone can join the masses of North Americans who are returning to the outdoor garden. This book will offer inspiration and instruction for both the beginner and more advanced gardener. If you've got earth to plant in, this book will hold your hand through the process. I welcome you to a world where fingernails get dirty and thumbs turn green.

Chapter 1

LOCATION LOCATION LOCATION

In the spring, at the end of the day, you should smell like dirt. ~ Margaret Atwood

UNDERSTANDING YOUR LOCATION

If you've ever bought or sold a house, you know how important location is when talking real estate. One of the first homes we considered purchasing as newlyweds was this little bungalow plopped beside a small airport in Ontario. Thank goodness for a wise realtor who skillfully guided us away from that location. Imagine trying to get a newborn to nap with airplanes taking off at all hours, not to mention a later attempt at resale! Indeed, location is everything! The same is absolutely true of gardening. In order to achieve your dream landscape you will need to fully understand the location where you wish to plant.

While most people look to the ground for the perfect landscape locale, don't be afraid to think beyond the usual garden haunts. As people satisfy their hankering for greener lifestyles, window boxes, gutter gardens, hollowed out logs, roof-tops, and recycled containers are popping up all over the world as garden spots. A great thing about the container garden movement is that you can always relocate your garden if you find a plant not thriving in a particular spot.

When it comes to the more technical aspects, you needn't be an environmental engineer to do a quick assessment of your location. In fact, you can accomplish this in one day! You'll need to consider: **sunlight, soil and drainage.**

SUNLIGHT: How much and when?

First things first. You have a spectacular spot on the side of your house perfect for a garden filled with lush, flowering perennials. You run to the local greenhouse and purchase bashful hydrangeas and hearty hostas. After just one season, your hydrangeas' leaves are yellowed with blackened tips, and your hostas look like your hair after that perm you got in the eighth grade--fried! *Did you consider the amount of sun your garden would get?* In this case, the spot you chose had full sun while the plants you selected prefer a shadier environment, please and thank you.

You will have a location that has **dappled sun, partial shade/partial sun, full shade,** or **full sun.** Determining exactly what you have is really very simple.

Take the time to examine your location by considering the following questions about the sun:

1. Where is the sun first thing in the morning?

2. Where is the sun by noon?

3. Where is the sun by 4 PM?

4. What trees will block the sun seasonally when their leaves are out?

5. What structures will block the sun?

6. How will the season affect the trajectory of the sun in this location? (For example, some locations will get more sun later in the growing season as the sun is higher in the sky.)

Answering these questions will give you a ballpark idea of how many hours of sunlight your garden spot will get. *Generally speaking, plants boasting larger blooms or bearing fruit require around six to eight hours of sunlight per day. Conversely, plants producing small or no flowers but display lovely foliage tend to prefer more shade.* Those are general guidelines to keep in mind when you notice a plant you love, however garden centers and greenhouses usually tag their plants to let you know exactly what locale will best suit your plant. Pay attention to the labels-- they're a novice gardener's best friend.

WHAT DOES IT ALL MEAN?

So you've figured out how many hours of sunlight your garden spot will get, and you head to the garden center to select beautiful plants. Here's how to understand the greenhouse labels.

Full Sun

Between 6 and 8 hours of sunlight per day.

Partial Sun

Between 3 and 6 hours of sunlight per day (Though used interchangeably with *Partial Shade*, this plant will definitely need at least the minimum of 3 hours per day.)

Partial Shade

Between 3 and 6 hours of sunlight per day (Though used interchangeably with *Partial Sun*, this plant will definitely need relief from the hot, afternoon sunshine.)

Dappled Sunlight

Not as frequently seen on commercial plant labels, this term indicates the need for some type of filter--a large deciduous tree or other woodland shrubbery that causes intermittent moments of sunlight instead of a short period of steady light. The on again, off again filtered light causes the accumulated total amount of sun to be close to *Partial Shade*.

Full Shade

Less than 3 hours of sunlight per day.

You'll choose plants based on the number of hours of sunlight they receive. But before you *actually* select plants, let's talk soil.

SOIL: Time to get your hands dirty!

We've all heard of those crazy people who put coffee grounds around the base of their hydrangeas to change the color. To those of us who could drown a plant during a drought, they speak a foreign language filled with strange words like alkalinity and acidity. What? Fear not! Learning the type of soil you have is as simple as tossing a bit in a Ziploc bag and running up to your local Cooperative Extension office.

Hint: MOST PEOPLE SKIP THIS STEP

Big Mistake! Invest the time to go outside with a few bags and take samples from a variety of spots in your garden. Take your dirt from about three or four inches below the surface. You can then take these samples to the Cooperative Extension office in your county where they will test them for you free or for a minimal charge. (Need more info on locating your local extension office? No problem.

Classygroundcovers.com/site/page?view=cooperativeextensions has links to all the extension offices. If you are feeling adventurous, you can always purchase soil test kits at gardening centers and online at Amazon. They're not hard to use.

Beginner

For the novice gardener, you will want to determine what type of soil you actually have. Below, you will find the most common soil types and how to improve them. If the thought of testing and amending soil overwhelms you, follow the beginner's advice.

Advanced

If you are comfortable with more technical gardening, look at the advanced improvement options. (A complete list of Soil Improvers can be found below soil types.)

Measuring Soil Amenders

Most bulk sources of soil improvers are measured in cubic yards which is equal to 27 cubic feet. What you really need to know is that *1 cubic yard covers 100 square feet of area with roughly 3 inches of material (a 10 X 10 foot space).*

pH and Soil Tests. What's all the fuss?

Here's the lowdown on soil pH. Basically soil is just like the human body in that it needs an optimal pH balance to absorb nutrients effectively. The pH scale runs from 1-14 with 7 being neutral, below 7 being acid and above 7 being alkaline. And in case you wondered, acidic soils tend to be sour and alkaline soils tend to be sweet. Here's the real rub: *plants tend to love soil that ranges between a 6.2 and 7.2 pH level.* Often lime--a by-product of the mining industry made up of calcium or calcium and magnesium--is added to acidic soils and sulphur is added to alkaline soils to neutralize them both. Should you test? As a more advanced gardener, absolutely! The information you gain will prove highly beneficial as long as you act on it. Don't forget to use the following link to locate your extension office: classygroundcovers.com/site/page?view=cooperativeextensions

SOIL TYPES

1. Clay Soil

True to its name, when clay soil is wet, it will clump together in a ball similar to the clay a potter uses. When it is dry, it will form rock-like clumps or crack along the surface. On the plus side, clay soil tends to retain moisture and nutrients relatively well. On the negative side, in addition to a tendency toward being alkaline, clay soil can be so dense that plant roots have difficulty spreading out as they grow. (Don't freak out; we'll get to this.)

Improvements for clay soil:
Sedge Peat--Increases moisture absorption, and loosens clay soil.
Garden Compost, Aged Manure--Make sure you select aged manure because it offers better texture for clay,

will give additional nutrients to the soil, and won't
burn young plants.

Coarse Sand--Think sand from a builder's supply store,
not sandbox sand which is too fine. You want good grit.
It will loosen heavy, dense clay.

Conditioners for clay soil:

Calcified Seaweed--Will neutralize an acidic soil, and
break down clay soil.

Sulfur Chips--Will add acidity to a neutral or somewhat
alkaline soil.

Improvement Amounts:

Cut (mix into existing soil until well incorporated) 2-3
inches each of Sedge peat, compost/manure and sand)
into the clay.

Beginner

You may try skipping any soil improvements and
simply look for plants that thrive in clay. For example,
butterfly bushes absolutely loved the stubborn red clay of
a bank behind my Georgia home. Contact your local
extension office to find out what plants do well in your
area. If you want to improve the soil somewhat, go to the
garden center and purchase enough Sedge peat and
organic matter to cover your garden spot with 3 inches of
each. Then cut it into the soil.

Advanced

You will certainly want to add Sedge peat, organic
matter and coarse sand to your soil. Consider the addition

of soil conditioners which can be purchased at your local garden center. Follow packaging instructions. Additionally, you may wish to perform repeated soil testing to determine how your soil is being affected by the break-down and subsequent addition of nutrients due to the organic matter you have introduced. If you find your soil responds well, you may consider plants beyond those that are known for doing well in clay.

2. Silt

Somewhere between chalky and sandy soil in terms of texture, silt soil actually feels almost silky when you rub it between your fingers. Leaving a slight residue behind that will shine in sunlight, silty soil is rich in nutrients but tends to become dense and waterlogged when wet. Like sandy soil, silty soils warm more quickly in the spring offering a slightly earlier planting season.

Improvements for silty soil:
Organic Matter--Silty soil is rich in nutrients but can easily become water logged, so you will want to add organic matter such as compost and/or very well decayed wood shavings or sawdust.
Walkways--Silty soil can become compacted if stepped on repeatedly. If you must walk through your garden, consider adding walkways in the form of pavers, boards etc. as a regular pathway. Keeping your foot traffic in one area will prevent you from stepping too close to your plants' root systems.

Improvement Amounts:

Add approximately 6 inches of organic matter into soil.

Beginner

If you are just learning to garden and have no other location, then you will want to cut (mix into existing soil until well incorporated) in a large quantity of organic matter. If you need to purchase in bulk, stick to a supplier with a good reputation. If your garden is small enough to purchase your amendments at a garden center, look for organic matter that is not manure based. Remember to plan for about 6 inches total new matter that will be cut into the existing soil. Plan to use an all-purpose fertilizer regularly.

Advanced

This soil will need the addition of around 6 inches of organic matter. You may wish to combine a few different sources of organic matter. Mel Bartholomew, who wrote *The All New Square Foot Gardening*, suggests offering your garden a variety of different sources of compost/organic matter guarantees a variety of nutritional benefits. (97) In other words, don't buy all mushroom compost. You will want to regularly test your soil to examine the pH as well as salt levels. Silty soil lends itself to the addition of highly decayed wood shavings and saw dust, so you may save some money by stopping in at your local cabinet maker's shop where you can get a large amount of wood shavings to start composting. Never underestimate the power of considering local resources like this in terms of monetary savings and environmental benefits.

3. Sandy Soil

Often a much lighter shade of brown than woodland soils, this soil doesn't hold water because it is largely composed of sand. Ultimately, sand is comprised of tiny particles of broken rocks--a solid surface component that does not absorb nutrients. If you examine this soil following a rainfall, you will notice that the water drains immediately. Try to ball it in your hand. Rather than hold shape, it will crumble in your hands. This type of soil is very hard on plant life. You will need a very hearty, high drainage/low nutrient tolerant plant or much amending. However, there are some benefits to sandy soil. It warms earlier than more dense soil due to such high air flow--this means you may be able to put plants in earlier. Additionally, it offers good drainage and is very easy to work with when it comes time to amend or weed.

Improvements for sandy soil:
Organic Matter
To provide concentrated nutrition, this soil will need a high amount of organic matter. Often this soil is found in seaside locations yielding high salt levels which can be harmful to plant roots. Organic matter also tends to yield salt as it breaks down. Because of this, you may find it best to skip manure and opt for vegetarian matter such as aged grass clippings, leaf mold, mushroom compost or humus. Cloudlike in texture, fluffy humus will bind the soil together creating a better environment for nutrients and moisture to remain. If you have sandy soil, you should certainly consider the practice of composting which is discussed at length in chapter 5.

Vermiculite/Sphagnum Peat Moss—Both will offer moisture retention, but neither will address the nutrient concerns of this type of soil. Still, it is worth adding some of one or both because of long-term moisture retention benefits. If you are in a seaside locale, consider Sphagnum peat moss which offers lower salt levels than other peats.

Conditioner for sandy soil:

Lime—In sandy soil, the calcium content, which increases alkalinity is lessened because of leaching (drawing out of nutrients caused by the high drainage of sandy soil). This often results in an acid pH. As a result, it is worth testing pH levels and adding lime if necessary.

Improvement Amounts:

Add 1 inch of vermiculite/Sphagnum peat moss and around 5 inches of organic matter.

Beginner

Purchase at least two different types of aged, organic matter such as mushroom compost and one other plant based compost; cut the matter several inches into your soil.

Advanced

Cut in 5 parts of a mixture of 3 or more plant based varieties of aged, organic matter to 1 part either vermiculite or Sphagnum peat moss or a combination of both. Test your soil and determine pH. Purchase and apply

4. Chalky Soil

As the name suggests, chalky soil literally appears like chalk or drywall dust. When chalk rock is present, the soil will often have a whitish hue; you may even be able to view pure chalk. This soil is low on the nutrients spectrum and drains very easily.

Improvements for chalky soil:
Peat Moss--Will offer acidity and moisture absorption.
Aged Organic Matter--The need for nutrients in this soil is high. Adding bulky, aged organic matter will pay off in spades. Avoid mushroom compost as it tends toward alkalinity and will not improve your soil's pH level.

Conditioner for chalky soil:
Sulfur chips--Will increase acidity of the alkaline soil.

Improvement Amounts:
Add 3 inches each of peat and organic matter into soil.

Beginner

Consider a different location. If this location is your only option, you may wish to have a load of topsoil brought in and create a raised bed environment. You will need at least 5 inches of topsoil and 1 inch of aged organic matter. Alternatively, select plants that require little to no nutritional content and tolerate lower water retention.

Plan to regularly buy and use a good all-purpose fertilizer following package instructions.

Advanced

You have your work cut out for you, but you can amend this soil if you have no other location. Add at least 3 inches each of peat moss--which will address the alkalinity of chalky soil as well as increase moisture retention levels--and bulky, aged organic matter. Certainly consider the practice of composting (chapter 5) as you will need a steady supply of supplemental nutrients for this soil. Additionally, plan to add some sulfur chips to condition the soil, adding acidity. An all-purpose fertilizer will be highly beneficial if you are unable to regularly augment soil's nutritional content with good compost.

5. Peat

Though a rarity for garden spots, a purely peat soil is dark, like coffee grounds, in color, fibrous, and spongy. Peat will not hold shape when you attempt to make a ball. Because peat bogs tend to be acidic and hold water, they don't support a wide variety of plant life. There are many acid-loving plants that will thrive in this type of soil. Peat soils can become waterlogged. Lime will neutralize the acid pH making this soil more accommodating to a variety of plants. Because pure peat soils are not very common garden locales, we will not spend further time discussing them here.

6. Loam

Many soils are a combination of clay, sand, and silt. They may contain some chalky soil and even some peat. In general, loam soil will have a relatively even combination of the three main soil types. This equal representation of sand, silt, and clay makes loamy soil ideal for most garden plants. High in nutrients, but well-drained, loam also tends to offer a more balanced pH. Its texture is rich, relatively dark, and granular. If powdered sugar is silt, white sugar is sand, clay is brown sugar, then loam would be a mixture of all three.

Improvements for loam:
Organic Matter—Any soil can become depleted of nutrients over time, so a quality mixture of organic matter will benefit the soil in limited quantities.

Conditioner for loam:
Sulfur or Lime—The advanced gardener may wish to test this soil for pH and amend it with a bit of sulfur or lime accordingly.

Improvement Amounts:
Adding about 1 inch of organic matter per growing season will usually suffice.

Beginner
This is your lucky day. Run with it, and plan to add organic matter once every growing season.

Advanced

The advanced gardener may consider the practice of composting (chapter 5) as the addition of healthy compost to this soil will be the perfect nutritional supplement. Annually, the addition of some well-aged organic matter will certainly benefit loamy soil. If your loam swings toward one particular soil, you may wish to moderately amend according to that soil's improvement instructions. For example, a more clay-like loam will benefit from a Sedge peat, some coarse sand, and a bit of organic matter. Again, if you notice your soil tends to contain a higher concentration of one soil structure, by all means test the soil and amend it according to that soil type's recommended improvements as listed above.

A Soil Conditioner to Consider for the ADVANCED gardener: Gypsum

Touted as the universal soil amender, gypsum (calcium sulfate) is often recommended as a soil additive though research is still out, so cold hard facts are hard come by. That said, reliable garden centers such as Home Depot do recommend it for use with clay soil. It should break up the clay and create a clustering effect where air pockets are formed causing better circulation. For salty locations, gypsum is said to remove sodium replacing it with calcium. For the advanced gardener, all early evidence indicates gypsum may indeed be worth examining. For a more exhaustive discussion on the boasted benefits of its use simply type the term into Google and join the fray.

Final Thoughts on Soil: A Confession

I'd be crazy to give you all this information without being entirely honest. Really, I couldn't sleep at night if I didn't tell you that my favorite way to garden is to ignore the soil entirely. If your garden area isn't overly large, you have a little money to invest, and you don't mind learning to compost, I'd highly recommend you consider the author of *All New Square Foot Gardening,* Mel Bartholomew's approach. Buy his book if you have any intention of growing a single vegetable. In short, he recommends building *up* your soil with a mixture of 1/3 blended compost (several varieties), 1/3 peat moss, and 1/3 course vermiculite or perlite. (89) The idea is that you will establish between 6-12 inches of this "new soil" mix (which actually isn't soil at all) on top of your existing soil. Done properly, and let's face it, this isn't hard, you will reap the benefits of your investment almost immediately. How? Well, this particular combination just works. (Buy his book if you want the full rundown on why.)

For the beginner, I couldn't recommend this strongly enough. For the advanced gardener, you already know the challenges soil can offer, and while you may enjoy that challenge, this always friable, easily workable, nutrient rich soil will free you up to pursue more persnickety aspects of gardening. Granted there are locations where this approach isn't an option, and for those areas, you've got plenty of info above to help you along. But in smaller spaces, this is a very doable option, especially for timid gardeners just getting their feet wet. I used this approach with a large set of square foot gardens that included annual and perennial flowers, herbs and vegetables. I started countless plants from seed in this soil as well as planted things directly from containers. Not one single thing ever died, and my gardens were the envy of everyone who saw them.

DRAINAGE: Just how wet will your plants' feet be?

Typically, plants are sort of like people. They may enjoy an occasional relaxing soak on a spa day, but generally speaking, they don't want to spend too much time with their roots lingering in water. Therefore, your ideal location will offer good drainage. How can you tell if you have good drainage, you ask? Great question.

Beginner
1. Examine the existing plants.

Take a look around your location. Does it resemble an abandoned lot in the corner of the city somewhere, or is it more akin to a jungle environment with lush, overgrown greenery? These clues will tell you whether vegetation likes the location. Regardless if what you see are weeds, existing perennials, or grass, if they are thriving, the soil is likely well-drained and rich.

2. Dance in the rain.

Well, not literally. But do go out after a good long rain and observe your soil. Are there pools or puddles of water? If so, how long do they remain? These indicate that you have poorly drained soil. If the soil remains soggy for several days, you'll want to select plants that don't mind wet feet. If the soil dries out more quickly than the surrounding areas, you may need to select plants that will not mind. If the soil seems to steadily dry out over time, you've got a good spot for a variety of plants.

Advanced

So you're really into understanding your soil? Here are a few more technical approaches to learning about the drainage in your location.

1. Check for earthworms.

They don't appreciate poorly drained soil

2. Examine the texture of your soil.

The texture will let you know just how extreme your drainage conditions may be. It is not impossible to alter the texture to create an environment conducive to the plants you wish to grow, but it will mean that you need to amend the soil.

Sandy, loamy, and chalky soils tend to have very speedy drainage. You will need to consider amending them by cutting in large amounts of aged, organic matter and peat or sedge moss if you plan to use a variety of plants.

Heavy, dense soils tend to hold moisture. You will need to amend them by cutting in amounts of sedge peat, aged organic matter, and even coarse sand to loosen the soil, if you plan to use a variety of plants.

3. What color is your soil?

The color of your soil will tell you much about it in terms of both drainage and nutrient richness. Here is a general guideline to follow:

- Dark-rich brown/rusty soil

High amount of organic matter generally offering nice drainage and good nutrients (Most plants will love this environment.)

- Streaked soil
This soil can sometimes indicate variations in moisture levels which may mean extra water during hot seasons. (Choose hearty plants or plan to water seasonally, set up a sprinkler, or install a drip watering system.)

- Grey soil
This soil (often seen in clay) tends to be poorly drained. (Choose plants that don't mind wet feet.)

- Yellow soil
Usually this soil offers less than ideal drainage. (Choose hearty, tolerant plants, and be prepared to water, install a sprinkler, or drip watering system.)

4. Dig a hole
Understanding exactly how much water drains per hour will give you hard, fast information with which to determine if you need to amend your soil, select different plants, or a combination of both. Grab your shovel and dig a 12 inch hole. Fill it with water; allow it to drain fully. (Yep, you'll need to hang around and keep an eye on that hole.) When it has drained, fill it again, and measure the depth of water with a ruler. Jot that down and return in fifteen minutes to measure the depth of water. According to Cornell University's gardening website, you will take the difference from the two totals (or drop in water) and multiply it by 4 to learn the inches drained per hour. (gardening.cornell.edu)

Now that you know how many inches drain per hour, consider the following:

- Less than one inch per hour
Poor drainage, consider plants that don't mind soggy feet. Improvements: Consider amending with a combination of coarse sand, sedge peat, and aged organic matter.

- 2 to 6 inches per hour
Nice drainage. Most plants will do well in this environment provided the soil is also good.

- 6 to 12 inches per hour
Fast draining soil. Select plants that don't mind a drier environment. Consider amending with a combination of peat moss and aged organic matter as well as a top coat of mulch.

A Quick Review

So we had to sludge through quite a bit of material there. Ultimately though, understanding your soil is very straight forward. Don't be intimidated by lots of information. Take the information one step at a time. All great gardeners began with their first attempt. Many fail, but most surprise themselves and grow something beautiful. Here's a quick recap.

1. **Look at the Light**—A few trips outside throughout the day will give you a good idea how much light your location gets. Then you can label your spot as: *Dappled, Full Sun, Full Shade, Part Sun/Part Shade.*

2. **Sift the Soil**—A few bags of dirt and a shovel will help determine if you have: *Clay, Sand, Silt, Chalk, Peat, Loam.*

3. **Dig to Determine Drainage**—One quick shovel and a measurement or two with the ruler after filling a hole with some water gives you an idea if your soil drainage is: *Poor, Moderate, or Well-drained.*

Now What?

Now that you've determined what amount of sun your location gets, you've deciphered all that soil stuff, and even figured out how well-drained the area is . . . well, you deserve a medal. But additionally, you're ready to make a few decisions.

First of all, what plants do you long to place in your new garden? If a cutting of your grandmother's wisteria will be the backdrop for your garden, and your soil is a clump of grey clay, you'll need to amend the soil or plant Granny's wisteria somewhere else. Will you tweak your plants to suit your soil or tweak your soil to suit your dream plants? And be ruthlessly honest here. Your full shade location will not encourage Granny's wisteria to blossom, so don't "go ahead and try it." If the plant requires sun, and you have shade, change your plant or change your location. You'll be disappointed if you don't.

Secondly, will you amend the soil? Most likely you will decide you need to at least add some organic matter to your soil, and more likely than that, you've already priced out the cost of peat moss and a load of aged manure. Good for you! Go treat your soil. Prep the area. Remember the goal of soil amending is to create an environment where the plants will thrive long-term, so unless you are making a raised bed, *cut (incorporate thoroughly) the additional matter into your existing soil.* Take the time to mix it thoroughly offering a uniform bed for your new plants.

Now that you've waded through the mire of location issues and thought through the resulting ramifications for your garden, the real fun begins.

Chapter 2

THE FUN PART

Earth laughs in flowers. ~ Ralph Waldo Emerson

We all have our favorite plants. From blazing orange daylilies to creamy antique roses to leathery Baltic ivies, plants are as representative of our personalities as the paint colors we choose to dress the walls of our homes. Selecting plants is accessorizing our outside space. The more thought and care we put into it, the more we will adore the results when they thrive.

We've already established that any garden location offers unique benefits and challenges. Therefore, not all plants will thrive in all locations. Hostas, though lush and jungle-like just do not love unprotected, full-sun locations. So, if you're dealing with a southern exposure bed beside an asphalt driveway, I can guarantee you will be sorely disappointed with a Filigree hosta.

That said, because we can amend soil, and you've probably already done so, we do have some wiggle room. Here are a few questions to ask yourself which should help you determine just exactly what you are looking for.

PERFECT: Follow this acronym for the *perfect* plants.

P~rice~

I know; none of us really want to consider the *budget*--yuck! But you'll need to determine how much money you plan to invest in this project and research where you can get the best value for your dollar. Nowadays the internet offers some phenomenal garden centers at very affordable prices. Consider sites such as Classy Groundcovers (classygroundcovers.com) for countless affordable, perennial groundcover options including ivies, vincas, and even daylilies.

There are seasonal sales at local home garden stores, and don't be afraid to stop in on your neighbor and drop a rather heavy hint that you're in love with her phlox and long to have a tiny bit if she's considering dividing it this spring. (Showing up with a shovel and a plate of muffins won't hurt your chances!)

Additionally, check out the **Plant Scout** (davesgarden.com/products/ps) which offers a quick way to find vendors selling plants you seek.

Be sure to check reviews in the **Garden Watchdog** section before you buy! (davesgarden.com/products/gwd/)

Existing Interior Décor

The inside of your home will give you the best insight into the type of look and feel you will love the most in your garden area.

- Are you a rustic, country kind of gal with vintage roosters and chipped painted furniture?
- Are you a modern, urban gentleman with stainless counters and whale-grey walls?
- Are you a lover of all things Victorian?
- Are you an eclectic mixture of Bohemian hippy inspired tapestries and Target home décor?
- What colors fill your home now?
- How much color do you like? While some people want a fantasia of profuse color, others prefer only whites and greens hoping to achieve a more Zen feeling.

All of these answers will help you decide what you will most likely enjoy in an outdoor space. Most people don't stop to consider the reality that their decorative preferences extend beyond interior design. As a result, they often end up with a landscape that reflects the current trends from Lowes or Home Depot and not their own individual style.

Relax in the Garden Spot

Take a half hour to relax in the space with a garden book full of photos. Look at the photos of mature plants; try to envision them in the environment. Would the climbing hydrangea run out of space to climb? Would the bleeding heart be the perfect height against the small white picket fence that borders the garden? If you don't have a garden book, bring your laptop or smartphone with you and surf around on **Dave's Garden** (davesgarden.com), the premiere resource for gardeners who seek information or just want to share and expand their love of gardening.

While you sit in your garden, tour through the extensive **Guides & Information Area,** where you'll find the largest plant database in the world: **PlantFiles.** (davesgarden.com/guides/pf) Wonder how St. John's Wort does in clay? You'll find the answer you need here. This is a truly valuable resource at your fingertips.

Flip Through Garden Magazines

Leaf through a few different garden magazines and pull out every photo you like. Then lay all the photos out and look for an overall theme. How are they similar? What is it that captures you about all of them? Do you see purple on every page? Do you see varied textures in all different shades of green repeated? These themes will be the keys to a design you will love for years to come.

Etch-a-Sketch

Make a rough sketch of your garden with color pencils, using the theme, colors, and plants you like most attempting to keep the sketch to scale with plants at their mature size. How does it feel? Will there really be room for both a butterfly bush and forsythia in that four foot space? Drawing the garden will help you visualize what you are planning.

Consider the Seasons

Consider the plants' performance during all four seasons. How will this garden look in the fall when leaves begin to change color and blossoms lessen? How will it appear in the winter? Should you consider Helleborus for a late January, early February blossom when the rest of the garden is still sleeping? If you aren't sure about how your plants will look at different times of the year, hop online to Dave's Garden and look through his **Plant Files** section again. If all else fails, Google offers limitless images to help you see what your plant will do in various seasons.

Trust Your Gut

Gardening and life are similar in that you must learn to trust your gut. If you absolutely love it and the sun/shade works for the plant, go for it. This space reflects who you are--your soul even-- don't be afraid to plant what inspires you. You will spend much more time in the space if it holds the flora and fauna you adore.

Time to Make Your List

You're ready to choose. You've thought about this long and hard from just about every angle. Here's a final list of questions to ask yourself about each of your final selections followed by some last minute advice for both the beginner and the more advanced green thumbs.

1. Do I have the proper sunlight for the plant?
2. Do I have the proper soil for this plant?
3. Can my watering capabilities support this plant?
4. What height will the plant be at maturity?
5. What will the foliage look like?
6. What color blooms will it display?
7. When will it bloom?

A thorough, excellent website for selecting plants based on specific criteria like full sun, poor drainage, and clay soil is: classygroundcovers.com. You simply select attributes that may affect your plant, and their database generates all the plants they sell that will suit your needs. In addition, you can also use their handy Plant Calculator to determine exactly how many plants you will need for your square footage. (classygroundcovers.com/site/page?view=plantCalculator)

Beginner: Variety Really Is the Spice of Garden Life

Variety in a garden is paramount to achieving the look and feel you desire Gardens tend to offer the most visual appeal with a mixture of low, medium and high plants. Additionally, gardens are most pleasing to the eye when plants are clustered in odd numbered groupings. While some people opt for all one color blossoms, others prefer a variety of shades of foliage and flowers creating a different dynamic. Don't be afraid to experiment, but keep in mind the **PERFECT** plan for finding plants you will love.

Advanced: I've Got All That, Give Me a Challenge

For the gardener itching for greater challenge, have you ever noticed the most delightful gardens boast blooms throughout the seasons? Take the time to select plants that will flower at different times creating year-round interest.

For example, bittersweet vine offers delicate lacey-white blossoms in spring, glorious greenery in summer, vivid burnt red leaves in autumn and pumpkin orange berries to tempt birds in winter. Such a plant will do well paired with purple coneflower who promises deep purple blossoms in summer to accentuate bittersweet's jungle-green. And while the coneflower offers a nice height to your design, because Autumn Joy is a lower growing plant, including it will give the eye something interesting to view closer to the ground. Additionally, this sedum offers a succulent change of pace in foliage and a gorgeous late summer, early autumn mauve blossom. This combination of plants also offers birds something to munch on and will attract butterflies. You can see how taking the time to consider your plant fully makes a significant impact on the overall outcome of your garden. Ask these important questions of every plant. In the end, a garden should offer some beauty year-round.

A Word about Annuals

The first time I planted real plants in a garden, they were annuals. My seeds had been a dismal failure, knocking my budding garden ego back a few notches. I felt the best option was a flat of the bright smiling impatiens *already in bloom* in plentiful, economic containers at the local market. I amended the soil in a small corner garden by a shed where the sunlight was dappled by a large maple tree. The impatiens promised to grow in said spot. Indeed, they did grow! A gorgeous coral sunrise melted across that corner of our yard in Ontario all season long.

Don't turn your nose up at the annual flower. Annuals are a perfect beginner plant because they tend to be hearty, and their blooms offer immediate gratification giving you the needed courage to move onto bigger, better things. For the advanced gardener, annuals offer a sprite of color when other perennials aren't flowering and fill that gap you noticed last summer, but still haven't found a perfect perennial for yet.

Once, I filled a shade garden in Ontario with hostas, ferns, bleeding hearts and lily of the valley. The display was lovely, but it took a few seasons before the lily of the valley filled in all the gaps between my young garden plants. To supplement, I planted white impatiens. Never forget that you can create the look of a century-old English garden with a few well chosen annuals even if your fledgling garden is really only one season along.

When to Plant my PERFECT plants?
Spring and fall are optimal planting times. Springtime planting offers a full growing season to get established before your plant faces his first winter. On the other hand, fall planting affords the chance for plants to spread their roots out before the warmth of the spring growing season. *In either case, the general rule of thumb to follow is to plant at least one week after the first frost in spring or two weeks prior to the first frost in autumn.*

If you are planting bare root plants, a plant shipped without soil and pots online suppliers offer at considerable savings to the consumer, you must plant them soon after delivery. Make sure you get them in the ground at least a month before your first frost in autumn. Here's a link to find out frost dates for your area: victoryseeds.com/frost.

Planting in summertime is possible, but you should be prepared to do lots of watering and a bit of babying. The warmer your climate, the more taxing a summer planting can be. We'll touch on this again in the next chapter.

Where to go to find my PERFECT plants?

Indeed, nowadays, that is the million dollar question. Though we touched briefly on this topic under **Price**, determining where to buy your plants deserves a bit more attention. First of all, you need to know that solid, reliable help is as readily available as a computer. **Dave's Garden** (davesgarden.com) is the best online resource for gardeners needing trustworthy information. This site is mentioned more than once in this book because it is truly a valuable resource for gardeners. If you are looking to buy online, you will definitely want to check out Dave's **Products & Sources** area because it contains two jewels that every gardener should know about:

1. The Garden Watchdog
(davesgarden.com/products/gwd)

This spot contains reviews by members of over 7,000 mail order gardening companies. *You should ALWAYS check reviews here before buying anything online or through mail order companies.* If you are a research-a-holic with loads of time, sift through all 7,000 reviews. However, if you're like me--eyes glaze over after the first fifteen--save yourself some time and keep it simple, consider only the companies listed in **The Watchdog 30**. These are the thirty top rated companies. You cannot go wrong buying from any of them. And in case you want me to spell it out for you, here are a few of my personal faves:

Classy Groundcovers (classygroundcovers.com)
Free shipping of quality plants.

Easy to Grow Bulbs (easytogrowbulbs.com)
Bulbs from Holland for warm gardens.

Onalee's Home-Grown Seeds (onaleeseeds.com)
Great source for quality seeds.

2. The PlantScout (davesgarden.com/products/ps)
What? I know I mentioned it earlier in this chapter, but really, this is an uber-quick way to find vendors of the plants you want. And remember, you can check reviews in the Garden Watchdog before you buy! We are talking fool-proof garden purchasing here, folks!

The **Guides & Information** area is seriously massive with the cherry on top of the sundae being the largest plant database in the world. You can get quick, clear, dependable info on just about any plant. Find that in **Plant Files**: (davesgarden.com/guides/pf).

The **Communities** area is also worth a quick tour. It offers:

* Hundreds of gardening discussion forums.
* Tens of thousands (Yep, you read that right!) of people trading plants and seeds.
* Thousands of entertaining gardening blogs and journals.

A word of caution: This website can be more than slightly addictive! Brew some coffee!

Let's face it, some of us need to touch, to smell, and see the plants we are purchasing in person before we take the plunge. If foraging through the worldwide web is not your preferred mode of garden shopping, call your local extension office or Chamber of Commerce to find out when the area Master Gardener's Club has their annual plant sale. They all do this, and you can glean not only incredible, hearty plants, but some valuable garden advice for your region too.

Until just a few years ago, local growers in our area pulled their old flatbed pick-up trucks up to the side of the road filled with whatever crop was in season. If you name it--corn, peaches, turnips--I've bought it out of the back of some overall clad farmer's F150. The plumpest peach I ever ate came from a truck filled with peaches sitting outside the local bank. Make a deposit and get peaches for cobbler all in one spot--time and money well spent.

Nowadays our small town has made the trendy plunge into the foray of farmer's markets cropping up all over North America. Complete with crafters, veggies, fruits and children chomping homemade banana muffins from the local mill, our Farmer's Market serves tomato sandwiches and a morning filled with inspiration for gardeners. And the best treasure of all? You guessed it. Gardeners sell their plants. Everyone needs to divide their plants periodically. Just last year I spent two Saturdays selling plants from my overgrown herb garden. Left to themselves, my herbs had staged a coup in my vegetable garden. The vegetables were succumbing. Enter a friend who was fund-raising for their mission trip to spend a year teaching jungle children in Ecuador and Voila! Motivation found. I decided to divide my herbs and sell them to help my friend. I'd never done this before, but it turned out I absolutely loved it.

Everyone who purchased my fresh red basil, feathery dill, and lush parsley got way more than a good deal on mature, healthy herbs ready to go into the ground. They got my advice, my experience and probably way more conversation than they ever cared to have! The point? Go to the farmer's markets in your area seasonally. People will sell you their plants. Cheap!

Last, but certainly not least, and frankly, the most common spots of all, the garden centers in your area. From the local grocery store to your home improvement store to greenhouse growers, you will find plants for sale. Here are a few tips for when you shop at garden centers:

Check the soil. If it isn't moist, leave the plant. You don't want plants that haven't been properly watered.

Check the plant. Look at the plant. Is it droopy and leggy? Leave it behind. It has been neglected, and you don't want to spend good money on withered plants.

Check the color. Look for perky plants with good coloring. Yellowed leaves usually indicate nutrient imbalances.

Check with the attendant. Ask the garden center attendant what they can tell you about the plant. They may have valuable insight into where it will thrive best based on their personal training, experience, or information other customers have given them.

Check on returns. Confirm their return policy.

The only thing left is to make your final list and go shopping. We'll talk planting in the next chapter.

Chapter 3

TUCKING THEM IN

Don't judge each day by the harvest you reap, but by the seeds you plant. ~ Robert Louis Stevenson

We've got this old white F150 that I love to hate. We've had to replace the engine and the transmission, yet she still keeps plodding along. It is never my pleasure to climb into her duck-taped bench seat and drive; she's clunky, cumbersome and not so cool in the summertime. But, I do indeed love to drive her to my favorite plant purchasing haunts, fill her bed with soil, roots, and leaves, and head home for an afternoon of garden therapy.

My very favorite spot here in Northern Georgia is off a little back road that climbs over hills splitting cow pastures along the way. Paved only a few years ago, it serves the people that choose to live on family land tucked into the corners of our small county. The sole reason you'll find someone on this road is if they live there. And someone does live on it. I don't know her name. I don't know what she looks like--I've never even seen her.

What I have seen are her plants. Every spring, as soon as the soil surrenders her slumber and plants poke high enough through the ground to be divided, a small population of various pots begins to fill the edge of the roadside. They start on an old bench, and spill over onto the surrounding ground. Hostas, ferns, herbs, rose campions, ornamental grasses, and so many other miscellaneous heirloom plants fill buckets, old planters, and any other plastic container readily available. Each plant has a small piece of cardboard sticking up out of it with a buck or two price scratched onto it in Sharpie.

There's a bag of recycled grocery store plastic bags hanging from the bench and an old red Folgers coffee can with a slit cut out of the lid. It's the honor system. Take what you want, put your money in the can, make change if you need to, and drive home. Some seasons I make 3 or 4 trips by this little spot. One year I bought so many plants I felt inclined to leave extra money and a note to thank her for stocking my gardens after we moved into a new home. Those plants never failed me.

No matter where you've purchased your plants, you'll need to get them in the ground quickly and there are a few steps you won't want to skip including when to plant, dealing with the root systems, watering, and mulching once plants are in the ground.

WHEN TO PLANT

The ideal times to plant are spring or fall. If you live in a northerly climate, a general guide is to plant in the spring whenever possible. This allows your plant a full growing season to establish itself before it is forced to endure the long, cold winters associated with northern climates. If you must plant in the fall, be prepared to mulch and fence the base of any trees you plant. Should you live in milder climates, you may wish to plant in the fall, and in some cases right through the winter. Fruit-bearing trees such as peaches tend to show more growth when they are planted in the autumn. Planting in the autumn allows roots to grow and establish themselves before the first full growing season, so when this is possible, certainly do so. However, a spring planting gives your plant the mild growing time of spring before the heat of summer. The least ideal time to plant is obviously the chill of winter (particularly in cold regions) and the heat of summer (particularly in hotter regions). Should you be forced to plant in summer, be prepared to faithfully water.

SHOULD I FERTILIZE WHEN PLANTING?

You've already amended your garden spot according to your soil type, but you've heard you should add a fertilizer to the soil. You saw an entire aisle dedicated to colorful bags of pellets, crystals and liquids-- vitamins for your plants. Who can go wrong with a multi-vitamin, right? Well, you've done a lot of work to prepare your soil. Provided you've done your job, you shouldn't need a fertilizer when you put your plants in. If you're planting in the spring, your plants should do well in the climate you've created. In the fall, you'll want to revisit this. If you're planting in the fall, your plants should winter well. You may revisit fertilizing in the spring. Of course you will read fertilizer packaging labels, plant labels, blogs online, and standard-issue-expert advice that will suggest otherwise, and it is entirely up to you, but keep in mind that you can have too much of a good thing.

If your soil has been amended and tests well, trust the process. That said, your plants are hungriest during growing season when they are not only stretching their stems, they're developing foliage, buds and blooms. During this time, most garden experts say there are definite benefits to fertilizing every 4-6 weeks. You may wish to select a standard 10-10-10 fertilizer or something more specific to your plant. For example, there are specific fertilizers formulated for rose or rhododendron plants. With advancements in science, you will also find time released formulas that work for the entire season. Take your time as you peruse the fertilizer aisle in your garden center. Always follow manufacturer instructions and *never* use more than the package recommends as your plants can be burned as a result. For a more in depth discussion of fertilizing options, see chapter 4.

ROOT SYSTEMS AND BARE ROOT PLANTS
You are entering into the downhill portion of beginning your garden. The brain work has been done,

and now you'll enjoy the fruit of your labor in preparing a perfect bed. Carefully remove your plants from the container in which they arrived. You will be able to tell if your plant has become pot or root bound if the plant comes out in one full piece in the shape of your pot with roots surrounding the exterior. In this case, you will need to gently loosen the roots so that they are ready to spread down into the soil. When purchasing from big box nurseries, it is not uncommon to find this to be true. In fact, there will be some instances where you'll actually need a knife to break up the roots slightly.

If you have purchased bare root plants from an online supplier, this will not be an issue. But know this: **If you have bare root plants, it is imperative that you keep them moist until you plant them (but do not soak them in water).**

DIG
Dig a hole that is 2 times wider and deeper than the root

mass. For example, a root 3 inches deep and 1 1/2 inches wide requires a hole 6 inches deep and 3 inches wide.

LOOSEN

Break up the soil at the bottom of the hole so the roots can grow downward more easily.

PLANT

Set a plant in the hole. Plan ahead and leave room to collect rain water: the green stems should be about 1 inch below the level of the soil level, even more if you are on a slope.

FILL

Loosely drop in soil around the plant, fill the hole about 3/4 of the way.

LIFT

Assuming that your plant does not have fragile stems, grip the base of the stems and lift up the plant approximately 1/2 an inch. Gently push the soil down around the edges of the hole to compact it slightly. Do not pack it hard, just enough to remove large pockets of air (where water could pool and freeze, possibly damaging the roots).

FORM BOWL

Add more soil if needed, forming a bowl around the base of the plant to collect water. These plants are on a slope, and the bowl should be perpendicular to gravity, so the bowl is mounded on the downhill side and cut deep on the uphill side. This collects runoff, and the roots get more water.

WATER: Give Them a Drink

To encourage healthy root systems, you will want to water your plants evenly, especially during the first growing season. Between rain water and supplemental watering, *most plants will thrive with about one inch of water per week while they are becoming established.* Obviously there are more drought tolerant plants and more thirsty plants, but this is a good rule of thumb. Keeping the water consistent encourages the roots to dig deep into soil and establish themselves. Many gardeners suggest early morning watering so that the sunlight dries out the foliage preventing molds from growing in areas where water might otherwise sit if left overnight.

Of course many people employ sprinkler systems, do-it-yourself drip water systems, and other methods to hydrate their plants. Websites such as rainbird.com offer a plethora of watering options, many of which are very affordable. I have used a combination of sprinklers, hose attachments, and so on throughout the years. From a conservation standpoint, it merits mentioning that the purchase of one or two rain barrels with faucets attached will go a long way towards watering your plants.

MULCH: Give Them a Blanket

From pine straw to wood chips dyed ebony black, gardeners love mulch not only for its aesthetic beauty, but also for its practical uses. According to Donald Rakow,

> Many different natural and synthetic types of mulch are available today, but all perform at least three basic functions: *they reduce soil water losses, suppress weeds, and protect against temperature extremes.* In one study comparing various mulch materials with bare soil, soil moisture percentages in mulched plots were approximately twice as high, summer soil temperatures were reduced by 8 to 13 degrees, and the average amount of time required to remove weeds was reduced by two-thirds. (1)

Additionally, when using naturally occurring mulches, the garden gains the nutritional benefit of the material as it decomposes. And mulching helps prevent the crust that often forms on the surface of soil that inhibits moisture absorption. Compelling evidence in support of mulching, no doubt, but what should you use? From black plastic, to bark chips to stone, the possibilities--both natural and synthetic--are varied. Let's break them down and discuss the pros and cons of the most common options.

Bark Mulch

Most commercial bark chips are the by-product of firs, spruce and redwood trees. Though available in three standards, the most common and useful mulch for gardening is the bark chip (the largest chunks) because the weight and size of chips make them resistant to quick decay and less vulnerable to heavy rains or strong winds.

Pros:

Resistant to heavy rains

Resistant to decay

Resistant to strong winds

Cons:

Large chunks can float away

Pine Bark can lower soil pH slightly

Caution: While it may be tempting to use the free chips from your neighbor's recent clearing project, beware that chips who haven't aged properly may present toxins to your plants. It is best to select chips that have had time to stand.

Wood Chips

From your neighbor's wooded lot to the local mulch-yard, wood chips are often one of the most readily available options.

Pros:

Often FREE when municipalities stock-pile and allow people to take what they need

Economical even when purchased

Red Mulch (waste wood) can be dyed a variety of colors making them very attractive options

Cons:

Decays more quickly due to added sawdust content

May contain weed seed

Caution: Organic gardeners beware; wood chips may contain construction debris including pressure treated lumber pieces even when purchased from manufacturers.

Pine Straw

Because of affordability and availability, pine straw is becoming more and more popular particularly in gardens with acid loving plants.

Pros:

Affordable. Sometimes even free if you live near a pine grove

Readily available at most nurseries

Acid loving plants like azaleas and rhododendrons love this mulch

Cons:

Not good for plants that don't prefer high-acid environment

Not as uniform or easy to control aesthetically

Caution: Because of the acid content, pay attention to the pH level of your soil when using this type of mulch.

Pebbles/Stones/Shells

Certainly not suitable for all landscaping, but an excellent option for areas requiring a bold color statement, a permanent cover, or rock gardens.

Pros:

Long-term, won't decay

Choosing a solid color pebble can aesthetically enhance a garden

Water drains easily through stones

Cons:

Not easy to move

Pebbles may mix into soil over time

Not the most cost effective

Not suitable for all landscapes

Yard Clippings/Waste

From the cinnamon-brown maple leaves in autumn to spring and summer's extensive grass clippings, the often discarded or burned yard waste is a gold-mine of mulch.

Pros:

Who doesn't love FREE?

Readily available

Easy to transport

Excellent for plants requiring a mulching in the autumn because it offers the added benefit of nutrients as it decomposes

Cons:

Not attractive as an aesthetic addition to a garden
Not a long-term mulch due to decomposition
May have weed seeds

Recycled Tires

Not for every gardener, but for those desiring to make a green statement in addition to a strong color statement, recycled tires offer long-term bang for your initial buck.

Pros:
Who doesn't love recycled materials?
Won't break down
Bold color statement
Animals/insects don't care for it
Cons:
Let's face it, tires don't smell good
Tires are not the most economic option

Landscape Fabrics/Plastic

Because they offer two big wins for the garden--moisture retention and weed prevention--often professionally landscaped homes feature these sorts of "under-mulchings" blanketed with more aesthetically pleasing mulch on top. As a weed suppressant, I've even seen shingles or carpet scraps used!

Pros:
Retain moisture
Prevent weed growth

Economical

Cons:

Can cause root rot if material isn't porous enough

Prevent weeds from growing, but also make it impossible to use a creeping groundcover

Requires a top-dressing of mulch to look nice

Challenging (must cut into it) to plant other plants once they are down

BOTTOM LINE WHEN IT COMES TO MULCH

Beginner: It's Not That Big a Deal

If you are just entering the world of gardening, and cost is a consideration, go with a basic bark mulch that will offer you relative economy coupled with longevity. Choose a color that will offer contrast to the plants and your house.

Some like to think of the mulch as you would the carpet in your home. But remember too that mulching is not imperative and a well treated, rich soil is a lovely contrast to the lush green foliage of happy plants. Additionally, consider a creeping groundcover as opposed to traditional mulch. Why? First of all, it is a GREEN option. Second of all, an evergreen groundcover such as Vinca or Baltic Ivy provides not only year-round protection, but year-round beauty too. And third? Once established, a creeping groundcover does not need to be replaced or replenished periodically yielding an economic benefit as well.

ADVANCED: Of Course It Can Be a Big Deal If You Want!

If this is not your first rodeo, then you know that mulching offers its own set of challenges and benefits. Moving the mulch when you plant additional items or decide you don't like the existing arrangement in the garden can be an added step in your labor.

You also know that most mulch requires periodic replenishing. However, mulching can add nutrients/acids etc. to your garden. This can mean re-testing soil periodically--especially if you use an unknown mulch or pine straw etc. Why not try using some pine straw around your hydrangea to experiment with tweaking the color of her blooms? And it is a terrific idea to use it around your azaleas as an organic alternative to chemical fertilizers/conditioners offering greater acid.

When selecting your mulch, ask your garden center expert how the mulch will affect your soil. The bottom line for more advanced gardeners is that mulching can mean much more than just how your garden will appear. It can also be a fun way to experiment with tweaking the soil using various organic options. That said, my favorite groundcover is a live one. I highly recommend perusing the internet for innovative creeping groundcovers to cover your soil. From succulent sedums to flannel, creeping thymes, plants are by far the most delightful choices.

Chapter 4

FEEDING FRENZY: FERTILIZER

Why try to explain miracles to your kids when you can just have them plant a garden. ~ Robert Brault

Just as human beings who have a relatively stable, healthy diet still take vitamins, plants in a relatively healthy soil will still benefit from fertilizers. But remember this: Your plant's greatest ally is a well amended soil, *not Miracle Grow!* And also keep in mind that your plant *does make its own food* through the process of photosynthesis. (Remember fifth grade science class?) That being said, the standard fertilizer is a 10-10-10. But just what do those numbers really mean? Well, for starters, those numbers have a name: **Analysis**. That's what they're called.

The analysis lets you know exactly what that bag of pellets will offer your plants. These three numbers represent the major nutrients necessary for plant growth. Think of them as the food pyramid of plants. Just like we need a certain amount of fruits, protein and grains, plants need **nitrogen, phosphorus** and **potassium** to grow and thrive. Okay, before you newbies tuck tail and run, I will break this down for you in bite size pieces. You can do this! Promise. Just how exactly does this "analysis" affect your plants?

Beginner

If you are new to the world of gardening and all this scientific/gardening lingo is causing your head to spin, then simply purchase a 10-10-10 or 10-15-10 analysis fertilizer in pellet or crystal form at the garden center and follow packaging instructions when you incorporate it into your soil. Remember that if you have amended your soil properly, you shouldn't need to incorporate fertilizer until the following season. Skip the extensive breakdown below, and return to it after you've cleared your head and are ready to learn how to encourage your Clematis to bloom more.

Advanced

First-Nitrogen

The first number represents nitrogen, the goddess of green! Have you ever driven past a house with a velvety lawn that looks like its photo should be in the dictionary beside the word green? Chances are the owners or landscape expert who tends their lawn have met the goddess of green--nitrogen. Golf courses know all about nitrogen too. Regular applications of nitrogen cause plants to grow tall and darken their green tremendously. Thus, if you seek great, lush green plants, pay special attention to the first number on the fertilizer bag.

Does my plant need nitrogen?

      If your otherwise well-watered, well-drained plant appears unhealthy, here are a few road signs that may indicate the need to test your soil for nitrogen levels:
- Yellowing foliage (chlorosis)
- Fading foliage--green is fading to a lighter shade
- Veins appear reddish

What about natural sources?

      Thinking you'd like to steer clear of synthetic fertilizers? If you are looking for a natural source of nitrogen, you'll want to fast forward to chapter 5 where we discuss composting in detail. Plants rich in nitrogen exhibit healthy green foliage, so a compost pile rich in leafy green material is going to offer your garden an excellent nitrogen supplement. Also try organic fertilizers available in garden centers.

Can I have too much nitrogen?

      Yes, you can indeed. Remember, if you have amended your soil properly, the levels should be terrific to start out. If your plant is in the proper sun/shade environment and is not flowering or producing fruit, there is a good chance the nitrogen content is too high. The solution is to water often and well and refrain from adding any additional nitrogen rich fertilizer.

Second--Phosphorus

      My personal favorite, phosphorus, is a root booster; she will keep your plant's feet firmly cemented in the ground. Because, in proper levels, she helps plants establish strong root systems, phosphorus actually ends up giving us what we all love--beautiful blooms. (Now you know why she's my favorite.) Most high phosphorus fertilizers will feature phrases like Bloom Booster on their labels. But here's the reality. *If your soil has been properly amended, the correct levels should already be present. Increasing phosphorus while leaving other levels the same will not ensure the promise of better blooms. The correct levels of phosphorus are what are important.* In his article *Nutrition Myths That Can Damage Your Crops,* Fred Hulme, Ph.D., says, "Growers have long believed that they need to use high-phosphorus fertilizers at planting and during the flowering period for sufficient root and flower growth. The fact is growers need to supply all plant parts with essential elements at required amounts to achieve optimal growth. If healthy flowers or roots are analyzed for nutrient content, not only is phosphorus present, but so are all the other essential elements" (everris.us.com) If testing reveals your soil deficient, you will want to supplement with a higher phosphorus fertilizer judiciously, especially as buds develop and blooming occurs.

Does my plant need phosphorus?
      Here are a few telltale signs your plant may be hungry for phosphorus. If you notice any of these signs, pick up a soil test to confirm your suspicions.
- Purplish hue to veins
- Leaves may appear less green and more blue/grey/purple
- The stalks will be thin/weak
- The plant appears shorter when compared to other healthy plants
- Minimal blooms and undersized fruit

What about natural sources?
      Many a Canadian and British gardener will tout the benefits of bone meal, and arguably, they do exist. And it's natural! But, at the price, there are other less expensive

options yielding better results. Rock phosphate provides a slow release phosphorus boost over time. But it will take at least a year to generate real results. It is best used in acid soil. Also try organic fertilizer blends readily available in garden centers.

Can I have too much phosphorus?

Yes, you can, which is why you shouldn't go crazy with a bloom boosting fertilizer without testing your soil to be certain you absolutely need this formula. High amounts of phosphorus will prevent the absorption of iron and zinc and may also cause shallow root systems. *Though a soil test may reveal adequate amounts of iron and zinc, the plant will exhibit symptoms revealing the deficiency because it is not absorbing those nutrients from the soil.* A yellowing between the leaf veins indicates a possible iron deficiency and a bleached out appearance of the tissue could point to low zinc levels. Plants who love acid, like blueberries and azaleas, will not appreciate high levels of phosphorus and may even die.

Third-Potassium

The average novice likely hasn't heard as much about the third number, but it definitely serves a variety of critical purposes including cell function and nutrient absorption. Potassium, in proper levels, helps plants deal with extreme cold and drought by assisting the root systems. Many say that potassium aids the stem system of plants, and while this is true, much of what you see above ground happens because of what is going on below the surface. The other thing potassium is known for is its ability to help plants deal with pests and disease. If your roses got eaten up by aphids, test your soil, and be ready to look for fertilizer with higher potassium content. For those of us with less scientific minds, it might help to think about that third number in the analysis like this: "When things are going to "pot" consider some **pot**assium."

Does my plant need potassium?
Wondering about potassium in your plant? Potassium deficiency can be confused with drought or wind scorch, so if it presents a few of these symptoms, you'll want to test your soil to confirm.
- Dark purple spots appear on backside of leaf
- Leaf tips may appear brownish or scorched and curled
- Yellowing between the leaf veins (chlorosis)
- Stunted growth or minimal fruit are also indicators
- Generally weakened response to frost, disease and other pests

What about natural sources?
According to garden-soil.com, the best source of organic Potassium comes from wood ashes. "About the only generally-available organic source of potash, this material is treasured by organic gardeners. Wood ashes contain about 6 percent potash, plus considerable lime. Before corn cobs were used industrially, the cobs were burned in huge piles. The resultant ashes were peculiarly rich in potash-up to 35 per cent. Almost any ash resulting from burning organic materials that contain some fiber should be a fair source of potash. Wood ashes are particularly good to use for adding potash to a compost heap." ("Analyzing, Improving and Amending Your Soil")
Do be aware that you are gaining lime along with this potassium, so if you have an alkaline soil, you may wish to consider an alternative. Bottom line? It isn't a bad idea to visit your local cabinet maker and ask for some of his sawdust. You can add it to your compost pile as well as

burn it down as a natural source of potassium. And if you are fortunate enough to have a wood burning fire place, by all means, SAVE THOSE ASHES!

Can I have too much potassium?

The short answer? Yes, you can. The long answer? Well, similar to phosphorus, excessive potassium in soil actually prevents the roots from absorbing critical nutrients. So the signs may indicate a deficiency in nitrogen (see description above), magnesium and manganese (a yellowing of leaves beginning near the veins which can result in complete death of the leaves). As with all the other critical nutrients, fertilizers are an option when the soil test reveals levels that are too low.

What Were Those #'s For Again?

Right, after all that, you can't even remember what the analysis stands for! I hear you. I use this handy little acrostic to help myself remember. **N**ever **P**lant **Pot**. What? You won't forget it now, will you? **N**itrogen. **P**hosphorus. **Pot**assium! It works! Nitrogen is your goddess of green, phosphorus keeps your plant's feet in the ground and potassium keeps everything scientific from going to pot! This stuff isn't all that hard, is it?

A Few More Tips

Feed in the Morning

Many old-time gardeners will tell you the best time of day for feeding your plants is the morning. Naturally, if you are doing a combination water/fertilizer solution, the morning is ideal because you want foliage on plants to dry out during the day. If it is a time-released formula, the timing is a moot point. However, make sure your garden is moist when you feed, especially when using crystals or pellets.

Consider Reducing The Amount of Fertilizer

You should always follow manufacturer instructions, but you may wish to consider halving the amount they recommend. Some gardeners argue that the chief aim of the manufacturer is to make money and therefore they recommend the maximum amounts a plant will tolerate before having adverse affects. It stands to reason that there is certainly no harm in attempting half-dose and observing how your plants perform before using the maximum amounts. At any rate, make sure you do not over-feed which can burn your plants. Make sure you don't put concentrated crystals directly on the roots or leaves of a plant, and watch closely to see how your plant responds. Fertilizing is supplemental feeding, so if your plants are healthy, lush and thriving, you may not need to fertilize at all.

FINAL WORD ON FERTILIZERS

Fertilizers have come an incredibly long way over the years. Consider time released pellets or crystals which will give your plant continual nutrition for longer periods of time. Additionally, take a good look at organic options because they are plentiful these days, but read the labels. Not all organic products are created equally. Some people prefer to put out a time released fertilizer in the spring and fall. Conversely, I had a dear neighbor in Georgia who, in her late seventies, relished piddling and puttering about in her garden daily. She used a liquid version attached to a hose diluting the concentrate with a steady stream of water. Every week she drug out her hose and fertilizer jug. Her plants were gorgeous.

Much of fertilizing is a combination of what works well for you, and what you find works well with your plants. Ultimately remember that fertilizing is a supplement you will give your plants because they are not getting all they need from the soil. It is *not* your plants' primary nutrition source.

Chapter 5

COMPOST: ORGANIC GOLD

Gardening requires lots of water - most of it in the form of perspiration. ~ Lou Erickson

The first time I tried my hand at composting, we lived in the city. Behind my toddling boys' playhouse, I had my husband build me a small aerated box for kitchen scraps and grass clippings. I was amazed at how simple the process really was, and frankly I loved not having wilted lettuce greens and slimy egg shells mucking up my garbage can--no more leaky Hefty bags dripping as my husband carried them out on garbage day. The produce was no longer rotting, it was transforming to what I like to call, *organic gold*. From apple cores to egg cartons to watermelon rinds, I carefully saved every scrap that might otherwise escape my kitchen.

These household discards would become a veritable feast for my backyard paradise in Canada. If we had a dry snap, we moistened the pile. About once a week my husband would turn the growing pile with a shovel, and eventually we had compost. My plants were thrilled. And frankly, I couldn't believe how much kitchen waste we had been throwing out without any thought.

Composting just isn't that difficult. And if you get into the habit, you're doing the environment a favor, reducing waste and rot in landfills, using a resource you already have yielding financial benefits, and increasing your chances of keeping your garden organic. Plants will benefit just as much from a good variety of compost as they will commercial fertilizers. According to *All New Square Foot Garden* by Mel Bartholomew:

> Compost is absolutely the best material in which to grow your plants. Good compost has all the nutrients needed for plant growth. It's lose and friable and easily worked. It holds lots of moisture yet drains well. It's easy to make yet hard to find. The best kind is homemade compost that you make in your own backyard. The worst kind is the single ingredient byproduct some company has produced and bagged. (92)

Here's what you'll need.

Compost House
This needn't be fancy. In fact, none of mine have ever been anything more than a contraption built with scraps of material we had on hand. One was an aerated

box, another was several wooden stakes in the ground with chicken fencing attached. There's a gentleman in our town that parks his white truck on the side of a well-traveled road and sells barrels. Many of them he adapts for rain and some for composting. I've seen metal barrels fitted with a turning mechanism that allows you to rotate the material inside with a cranking motion. I even had one friend who simply threw her stuff in a large pile on the ground. It was her son's job to go out and turn it over periodically with a shovel. Whatever works for you in your situation is completely fine. Keep in mind that you will need a location that allows you to turn it with ease as well as some way to keep hungry critters from robbing you of your gold.

Size

Bartholomew says the ideal size for a compost pile is somewhere between 3X3X3 and 4X4X4 feet. This allows for maximum bulk which causes the pile to heat up creating the perfect environment for tiny microorganisms to break down your organic matter. At the same time, it limits the pile from being so large that its mere size prevents airflow thus creating an environment where stinky rot occurs. (Bartholomew 94)

Contents

A lot of people are confused by this aspect of composting. *I promise; this is easy.*

Your compost pile is a gluten intolerant vegan with one exception, she likes eggshells, and isn't afraid to indulge in a bit of newspaper and chicken poop! The more variety you offer her, the more nutrition she will offer your plants. She will love you if you feed her the following:

* Go For It!

> Any scrap kitchen produce (Dice it up for quicker decomposing.)
> Egg shells (Break them up.)
> Egg Cartons (Tear them.)
> Paper towels/napkins (Take time to shred them.)
> Tea bags
> Stable or Poultry Manure
> Grass clippings (Allow them to dry out.)
> Dried leaves (My neighbors bag theirs for me.)
> Hay
> Newspapers (Take time to shred them.)
> Weeds (Make sure they have NOT gone to seed.)
> Old plants (Break them up.)

* Use Moderation!

> Wood shavings (My husband's a cabinet maker, so we have a steady supply. We don't put all of them in the compost.)
> Sawdust (See above.)
> Coffee grounds (Great, but highly acidic, so don't fill the entire pile with coffee grinds.)
> Pine needles (Same thing: Acidic, not too many.)
> Corn cobs (Break these up if you can.)
> Shredded tree parts (Bark, twigs, small branches.)

* No!

> Dog/Cat feces
> Cooked food (Some people use cooked veggies; I do not.)
> Meat
> Dairy/Cheese
> Eggs (Not the yolks, only egg shells.)
> Diseased plants
> Bones
> Cooked grains

Won't It Smell?

Nope. Not if you remember the following: Your compost pile DOES NOT want any dairy, no raw eggs, no dog or cat manure (too many diseases), no cooked food, no meat, no bones, no diseased plants, and no grains! It's really a piece of cake . . . or a tossed salad with no dressing. One time I had a very generous neighbor offer to help save me compost. For a few weeks, she saved all her kitchen scraps. All of them. Imagine the lurch of my stomach when I opened a large Rubbermaid bin she had reserved for me filled with salmon, brown rice, and well, most of it was unrecognizable, but the flies and smell? Those have remained forever etched in my mind. Your compost should *never* smell bad. And it won't if you stick to the list above.

Moisture

It's simple, really. You never want your pile to be soaked or waterlogged, and you never want it to suffer from thirst. If your compost is in a barrel, make sure there are air and drainage holes to promote air circulation, and drainage of excess moisture. Keep your pile moist. If it is crusty and crunchy, it is too dry. If you can squeeze moisture from it, it is definitely too wet. Often Mother Nature does a fine job of regulating the moisture content in your compost if it is exposed to rain, however, if Mother Nature is on strike or your pile is not open to rain water, you will need to occasionally give it a drink.

Turning

Make sure you rotate your compost. Whether it is in a pile and you must shovel it to move the center outside and the outside to the center or it is in a barrel that can be rotated, make sure that the contents are moved about regularly. In answer to the question of how frequently the compost should be turned, Bartholomew offers this rule of thumb, Turn "every day if you want the finished compost in two weeks; every week for results in three months; or every month for it to be ready in a year." (Bartholomew 93)

Beginner: Really? You think I can do that?

Yes, and frankly, you are CRAZY not to! Here's why. You already have these items in your home. They are FREE! Not only are they free, but you are doing the environment and your garbage can a major favor by composting them. In addition, it is rewarding. Promise!

So, here's what you'll do: Once your pile has become as dark as a Hershey bar and as rich as that commercial fertilizer they sell in stores, you'll simply work in a few scoops (think 2 coffee mugs full for small plants and 4 or 5 for large plants) to the soil surrounding your plant. If you remove a plant and put another in, add a mug full of your organic gold.

Advanced: You should already be doing this!
Come on now; if you are an advanced gardener, you already know the benefits of composting. Don't be lazy. Get out there and find the perfect spot for your pile. You will not regret this decision. The type of compost you will generate at your own home, from your own home's discarded organic matter will be far richer than what you purchase commercially because it will have such a variety of ingredients.

If you want some really technical benefits, consider this: according to earth911.com, composting introduces soil microorganisms including: bacteria, protozoa, actinomycetes, and fungi. They are not only found within compost, but proliferate within soil media. Microorganisms play an important role in organic matter decomposition which, in turn, leads to humus formation and nutrient availability. Microorganisms can also promote root activity as specific fungi work symbiotically with plant roots, assisting them in the extraction of nutrients from soils. Sufficient levels of organic matter also encourage the growth of earthworms, which through tunneling, increase water infiltration and aeration. (Mazzoni)

Everyone loves minimizing their carbon footprint. Keeping these scraps from entering our landfills where they will ultimately give off methane gas, the most damaging of all greenhouse gases, as they rot is certainly one way to give our environment some love. And if you are already composting and would like a challenge, have you tried worm compost yet? I dare you to look into it!

Final Thoughts on Composting

Composting is a year-round process. We are always saving our scraps and organic matter. Of course the pile freezes over in the winter, but we continue to add layer after layer. The warming of spring quickly takes care of winter's hoard. The ultimate benefits of composting are so significant that you really don't want to miss this easy gardening step. Many people get so carried away with composting that they actually stop into local restaurants, coffee shops, grocery stores and farmer's markets requesting their discarded produce, coffee grinds, etc. Additionally, don't forget the neighbor with the chicken coop and the girlfriend who has two horses and a cow leaving plops in the barn. These are perfect additions to your composting pile.

Ultimately, composting brings you a step closer to having full control over what goes into your garden. You *know* what is in your compost. Generally speaking, most of us can't even pronounce (let alone understand) what the ingredients on the back of commercial fertilizers mean. I have found over the years that my best gardens have always been the gardens where I augmented the soil nutritionally with compost as opposed to fertilizer. However, I will readily admit that there are definite times when utilizing a commercial fertilizer is not only helpful, but sometimes necessary and unavoidable. Nonetheless, why not begin creating your own organic gold and see if you don't find it rewarding and addictive?

Chapter 6

UNWELCOME INTRUDERS: HOW TO TACKLE PESTS AND DISEASE

The kiss of the sun for pardon,
The song of the birds for mirth,—
One is nearer God's heart in a garden
Than anywhere else on earth.
~ Dorothy Frances Gurney

"Each year North American homes use approximately 136 million pounds of pesticides on lawns and gardens, and in the home. In fact, homeowners use about three times the amount of pesticides as farmers. Most wildlife pest poisonings, and most surface water contamination from pesticides, come from single-family homes." ("Natural Garden Pest Control") It is astounding to me that the home gardener is responsible for the majority of water contamination from pesticides! While this is not a treatise on organic gardens, I'd be remiss if I didn't at least plug this option.

Having enjoyed an extensive, organic garden for many years, I can tell you with great confidence that many of the issues gardeners face are a result of chemical sprays. While they are not without value, chemical sprays will often kill more than the critters you wish to be rid of. On the other hand, a garden with bountiful trees, bird feeders, and patches of wild flowers will invite nature's predators who will often rid your precious roses of those pesky aphids. Plants have survived for centuries without mankind's help, propagating, reproducing, and flourishing. Therefore, nature must have a way of dealing with potential threats to your perennials. A few simple tricks will aid you in your war against garden pests and disease.

1. Let the Bees Go to Bed

Whatever pest control sprays you use, apply them in the evening. Bees have bedded down for the night and therefore will not be harmed. Bees are a gardener's dear friend.

2. Tidy Up

Keep your gardens tidy, ridding them of grass clippings, weeds, and any other debris that may offer a cozy habitat for egg-laying and homebuilding of pests. A tidy garden leaves less room for unwelcome guests to hide. Wash pots, containers and tools after use to keep from transferring any problems.

3. Burn Anything With a Persistent Problem.

Should you find a plant with a recurring issue, don't discard it in your compost pile. Instead, burn it, killing everything bad without harming the environment or your fragile garden ecosystem.

4. Wake Your Plants Up With Water

Water early so that your plants are dry for most of the day. Many experienced gardeners contend that early morning is the best time to give plants a drink allowing the sunshine to dry them off thus preventing mold and other fungus from growing on foliage.

5. Mix Plants

When vegetable gardening, crop rotation is a proven pest control option. However, in a perennial garden where you don't intend to move that hydrangea once she's set her roots, you may want to simply add a variety of other plants since many pests are plant specific. An entire bed of hostas is slug paradise, for example.

What Types of Organic Options Are Out There?

I remember well my first foray into organic pest control. Grandma Jean, my 71-year-old neighbor with gardens bearing century-old pink peonies the size of sandwich plates among other beautiful vintage flowers, swore by home remedies. One day I noticed Grandma Jean outside in her gardening shoes, kitchen cayenne pepper in hand. As she strategically sprinkled the red powder, I wondered if she had lost it. When I inquired, she grinned, squinted her eyes, and raised her left fist in fury. "Those squirrels think they're going to get my tulips. I've got a little surprise for them!" From shredded Irish Spring soap, to crushed eggshells and cayenne pepper, she used everyday ingredients to control all manner of pests from destroying her gardens. Never once did I see her use a pesticide, yet her gardens flourished.

These days the organic options are multiplying almost as quickly as weeds gone to seed! Not only do your local garden centers now carry a plethora of organic pest-control options, ideas abound on the internet too. Below I'll share a few that have worked well for me over the years in addition to other available options I've heard spoken well of. This is by no means an exhaustive list. On the contrary, consider this a tiny appetizer just to get your mind thinking. Organic gardening deserves its own book, but I can promise you that once you dip your toes in the organic gardening water, you'll want to go for a very long swim. It's that amazing! Below you'll find organic options beginning with pest fighting plants, then traps, sprays and even more bugs! As with the other chapters in this book, I've included selections for both beginner and more advanced gardeners.

Pest Fighting Plants

Beginner: Start with these two

Nasturtium

Gardening friend, please meet Nasturtium. I promise once you introduce them to your garden, you'll *never* want them to leave. They are like having house guests who clean daily for you! How perfect is that? Not only are these plants a playfully elegant addition to gardens, they're easy to grow from seed in most soils, and entirely edible. Lovely, scalloped, circular chalky-green leaves offer a pungent peppery addition to soups, salads and stir-fries. A fusion of vivid orange, rust, and yellow color the edible flowers. Even the seed pods of these plants can be used where capers are called for in recipes. Most importantly, these plants fight unwelcome pests. According to wikipedia.org, "Nasturtiums are also considered widely useful companion plants. They repel a great many cucurbit pests, like squash bugs, cucumber beetles, and several caterpillars. They have a similar range of benefits for brassica plants, especially broccoli and cauliflower. They also serve as a trap crop against black fly aphids. They also attract beneficial predatory insects." ("Tropaeolum majus")

All of my gardens make room for a few nasturtium plants. Annually, I plant them from seed and enjoy their quick growing foliage and flowers until the first hard frost. In healthy soil, nasturtium will grow several feet if given the chance, but will mind its manners if trimmed back. Really, though, I dare you to plant a few seeds in your tall planters or window boxes and let her cascade of color dazzle your neighbors. One year I neglected to purchase nasturtium seeds, and while I kept promising myself I'd order some organic seeds, I never remembered. The entire season went by without a single nasturtium plant in my garden. Boy did I pay. That was my worst year ever for pests. Put them near roses because their flowers serve as a trap for aphids. While annual in nature, they will re-seed themselves prolifically if left alone.

Marigolds

Everybody's heard about marigolds' stealth when it comes to fighting unwanted garden insects and rightly so. A garden that houses marigolds will certainly see less trouble from unwelcome visitors. From aphids to mosquitoes, marigolds' bold fragrance frightens pushy pests away. But not all insects are repelled. Grasshoppers, for example, don't seem to mind marigolds' strong odor. Known for her medicinal qualities, marigolds are annual flowers who, when planted from seed, will offer a lengthy blooming period around 2 months from the time they're put in the ground. A bit of regular dead-heading encourages further blooming. Though not regularly, I have experienced marigolds returning from the prior season's spent seeds, but I wouldn't count on this like you can with other annuals such as dill.

Both marigolds and nasturtium are fine placed in pots and planters if you don't have room in your garden bed. Careful placement of potted plants will work just as well for you.

ADVANCED: A longer list

Lavender

One perennial to always save room for is lavender. Purchase a few small lavender plants from your local greenhouse or start them from seed. Lavender offers stunning textural contrast to many bright greens with its soft grey tinged foliage. Its fragrance is lovely and it will not only dispel moths and fleas (some use her essential oil as an alternative flea treatment for pets), it will attract many helpful insects. The delicate blooms offer an abundance of herbal medicinal remedies should you decide to further explore.

Catnip

The great garden repellant (except for cats, that is), catnip will undoubtedly repel more mosquitoes than Deet, leaving your garden area a pleasure to stroll through in the evenings. In addition, well-placed catnip will deter cats from using the whole of your garden for their toilet purposes. (I know this from experience.) Some say mice and rats are also offended by her presence in your garden, so that in itself is something to consider. Additionally, aphids, Japanese beetles (my personal enemy), ants, squash bugs and more are not fond of catnip. Catnip can tend to grow beautifully and then collapse leaving a bald center; be prepared to give it an occasional trim to prevent this from happening.

Chives

If your roses have been affected by Japanese beetles, you may wish to put a clump of chives nearby. Known for repelling those hungry metallic bugs, chives give you another edible addition to the garden. People eat their blooms in addition to their infamous green stems.

Garlic

You've probably noticed by now than many insect repellant plants are also edible. That's largely due to the fact that herbs have such potent aroma, and their essential oils are so pungent that critters tend to be slightly appalled by them. Garlic (a member of the lily family) is no exception to this rule, and frankly, if you enjoy cooking, you should consider growing a few varieties of this hearty bulb. Harvesting is simple, the reward--delicious food--is undeniable, and the pest elimination assistance is well worth the effort. Of course I happen to adore garlic for her early green foliage that climbs tall in spring and later, her gorgeous purple and white floral balls are a perfect addition to gardens. We eat the flowers in stir-fries, salads and dressings.

Garlic is said to deter nuisances like aphids, codling moths--think apple maggots, beetles, and even snails. One year on a return visit to a market in Ontario, I found bulging bulbs of elephant garlic piled in a basket. On a whim, I bought a few of the lumps that were larger than my fist, took them home to the mountains of Georgia, and planted them. I wouldn't always recommend this, but I hadn't seen elephant garlic in my rural area of Appalachia. I was willing to give it a try. The first season I was blessed with elephant garlic, the second season, well . . . let's just say it was abundant, our immune systems were strong, and we chewed a lot of peppermint gum!

Petunias

Who doesn't enjoy having a few planters filled with these ruffled, rewarding flowers? Aphids don't. Neither do squash bugs or rose chafer. Go ahead; indulge in that flat of velvety petunias at the garden center. They'll reward you handsomely.

As I said, my intention is not to offer an extensive inquiry into pest reducing plants, but if your interest has been piqued, do check out these more extensive lists online: pallensmith.com/articles/pest-control-plants and wikipedia.org/wiki/List_of_repellent_plants.

Traps/Bait

From contraptions made out of coke cans and beer (apparently slugs like to get into the sauce!), to aphid bait, to Japanese beetle bags, there is a wide range of pesticide free traps that rid your perennials of pests. Here are a few to consider:

Beginner

Hang pie tins

If you drive through any rural area with gardens, you'll often notice shiny pie tins hanging from strings. Just like the good old scarecrow, this tactic works wonders with deer if they are a problem in your area.

Scarecrows

They're fun to make with the grandkids and they do indeed scare birds away.

Japanese beetle traps

I've seen Japanese beetles gorge themselves on so many plants--the worst of which was my mother's beautiful crepe myrtle. If they're hungry, it matters not what you have to offer; they'll eat it. Hang one of these pheromone filled bags at the far perimeter of your property to lure these despised bugs far from your garden plants.

Advanced

Slug jug

One of my favorites, creating a beer-filled slug pond will help rid your garden of one of the most destructive pests known to any green-thumb enthusiast. You can use a jar, a can or any other small container. Simply bury the container partially filled with beer up to its neck in the soil. If you have a large garden, a few of these, carefully placed, will entice those slugs to come in for a swim. They will drown. (You can purchase traps like this as well.) Alternatively you can use inverted melon rinds, grape fruit or orange halves placed upside down, and even old boards set down on the soil of your garden. In the morning, remove and destroy the visiting slugs.

Diatomaceous earth

Now this powdery dust is well worth familiarizing yourself with. The powdered skeletal remains of microscopic creatures, diatomaceous earth's tiny particles are jagged and deadly to soft bodied pests. Most effective when dry, though some do make a spray out of it, you'll find this most beneficial during dry seasons. If your garden is watered by a hose or sprinkler system, you will want to apply this powder when foliage is dry.

Pheromone traps

Briefly touched on above with the popular Japanese beetle traps, know that pheromone traps are available for a variety of garden pests. One tidbit about these traps: they're essentially cologne for critters and therefore, they attract more of the males than females. When you see traps filling up, it's a great sign that you've got that pest in your garden. You may still want to launch a secondary attack in your garden against such predators because the ladies will linger longer.

Fly Paper Gone Wild

Okay, remember when you were a wee child visiting Grandma? You walked into her house and there were these odd one inch amber bands hanging from the ceiling with black dots on them. Fly papers. Granny had flies and used one of the most effective remedies for keeping them away from the peas she was shelling and the pies she had cooling. Well, the same principles still apply to pests . . . even in the garden. Most commonly seen painted yellow, people will often take a board, paint it yellow, slather it with sticky goop like Tangle Trap which comes in spray and paintable varieties, and let it do the work of pest control for them.

Since various pests are attracted to various colors, organicgardening.com recommends the following:
- yellow traps attract whiteflies, fruit flies, male winged scales, leafhoppers, fungus gnats, midges, male winged mealybugs and leafminers, thrips, psyllids, and winged aphids
- white traps lure whiteflies, plant bugs, cucumber beetles, and flea beetles
- light blue traps attract flower thrips, and red spheres attract the flies whose eggs hatch into apple maggots. ("Organic Pest Control Techniques")

You can buy entire trap systems, but why not get the kids involved and build them yourself?

Create Your Own Spray

Beginner

Give your plants a bath

Most gardeners use this tried and true method at some point or other in their career. A solution of 1 tablespoon dishwashing soap mixed with 1 gallon of water works wonders on soft-backed creatures whose body cannot tolerate soap. Aphids, scale, mites, and thrips will not survive a good bath because their outer shell will dissolve. Ouch! Sorry, bugs.

Advanced

Baking soda spray

For fungal issues, this one should have a place in your repertoire. Combine 1 tablespoon each of baking soda, dishwashing soap, and vegetable oil with 1 gallon of water. The soda is what prevents the fungus from growing while the oil and soap help the mixture to adhere to your plants. If you've got a fungal problem, you'll need to do this weekly, but its effectiveness makes it worth the effort.

All-purpose spray

I've seen dozens of variations of this spray, and I've used many of them. Organicgardening.com offers a really good one. They say the following about their recipe: "This spray combines the repellent effects of garlic, onion, and hot pepper with the insecticidal and surfactant properties of soap. Keep in mind that sprays that contain soap may harm natural enemies and pollinating insects. Apply it only to prevent or ease a specific pest problem." Here's their recipe:

- Chop, grind, or liquefy one garlic bulb and one small onion.
- Add 1 teaspoon of powdered cayenne pepper and mix with 1 quart of water.
- Steep 1 hour, strain through cheesecloth.
- Add 1 tablespoon of liquid dish soap to the strained liquid; mix well.
- Spray your plants thoroughly, including leaf undersides. Store the mixture for up to 1 week in a labeled, covered container in the refrigerator. ("All-Purpose Insect Pest Spray")

The options for organic sprays are as diverse as the options for shrubs and bushes in a garden. Kelp fertilizer sprays are an over the counter product that many use for pest control with success as well. For a list of fifteen different organic sprays made with readily available ingredients, check out this article: tlc.howstuffworks.com/home/homemade-organic-gardening-sprays.htm.

Coverage

From inverted milk jugs to recycled Mason Jars to plastic covers, a bit of physical protection in the early growth days of your plants can not only offer shelter, it can also offer extra heat because of greenhouse effects. I debated categorizing these options as beginner or advanced and finally decided they are for *PIDDLERS*-- people who just enjoy messing around in their garden and have the time to piddle with a few different ideas.

Piddlers

Certainly when vegetable gardening, you'll want to consider these options, but for baby perennials, these are excellent choices as well.

Mason Jars

So you bought some bare root mondo grass and now you're worried about the rabbits? They were adorable to see Easter morning, but now that they are nibbling on your grass, they're not so cute. And then the deer--who wants to feed their perennials to the deer? A simple solution? Stop by Grandma's house and pick up all her old canning jars from the cellar, dust them off, and place them inverted over the plants. Typically these pest lanterns will give your plants the added protection they need until they are big enough to stand on their own. One word of caution: Be aware of the temperature as it can increase by up to 30 degrees inside one of those little jars. On warmer days, remove the jars before the sun gets too high in the sky. Your early morning and later evening hours are the most worrisome when it comes to pests.

Row Covers

There are dozens of products readily available when considering covering gardens. Again, if you are vegetable gardening in rows, these are excellent choices. If, however, you've got yourself a beautiful flower garden, you may consider a larger rendition birthed from the same concept.

My husband built me what I used to refer to as my garden wagon covers. Constructed from long slabs of one by two, basic hardware-store plastic in rolls, PVC pipe, and a few screws, he fashioned a cover shaped like the canvas coverings of wagons back when they settled the west. These stretched over my gardens providing extra warmth in springtime, protection from frost in the late fall, and protection from a variety of pests throughout the season. By simply attaching (with a staple gun) the plastic to the one by two boards, placing screws across from each other into the border of my gardens, hooking the PVC pipes onto the screws so that they formed the skeleton/ribs over which the plastic would stretch, and draping the plastic over the inverted, U-shaped PVC pipes, we had a greenhouse/pest protector for pennies! I could remove it when the weather was hot and put it back on in the evening and through the night to keep deer, rabbits, coons and other hungry mouths at bay. This could be adapted in a variety of ways to accommodate your garden.

Tomato Cage Covers

Similar to the concept above, if you've got small shrubs just taking off that need added protection, consider your everyday tomato cage. Place it around the shrub and wrap it in a light screen or plastic (garden centers offer a variety of webbing and other mesh materials as well) offering it necessary protection from intruding pests.

Get to Know the Good Guys

And if you are absolutely over the moon about all these organic ideas and find yourself wandering out to your gardens multiple times a day, you may just be the perfect candidate for this next option. Familiarize yourself with the bug, insect and critter kingdom! Get to know the good garden creatures. The list of creepy crawlies that actually prey on the not-so-nice ones is extensive. For example, praying mantis and ladybugs will feast on the bad guys offering your garden round the clock soldiering while you sip sweet tea on the sidelines. Just the other day while jogging, I noticed a praying mantis sack bulging from a small shrub on the side of the road. Instantly, I put on the brakes. That is a treasure chest for the gardener. Simply breaking off the stick and placing it in my garden where the eggs will hatch and release an army of prayerful soldiers guarantees my garden a level of organic protection. Of course if you aren't fortunate enough to stumble on a sac while jogging, order one online or stop by your local garden center.

You can also buy live ladybugs for the same purpose. These are very cost effective methods (gobs of ladybugs run around the twenty-five dollar range at Home Depot) that have proven effective for generations of gardeners. Parasitic nematodes offer similar benefits though they attack from within the insect once ingested. They too are readily available for purchase. Here is a more exhaustive list: eartheasy.com/grow_nat_pest_cntrl.htm.

Fascinated by this concept? Why not grow your own garden insectary? Check out this article: eartheasy.com/grow_garden_insectary.htm.

Additionally, there are both insecticidal and oil sprays commercially available as well as a plethora of other organic options at local garden centers. As I said beginning this chapter, my intent is to offer you a small sampling of organic options to get your mind going. If this venture into organic choices has your mind buzzing with ideas like a hive of bees, consider purchasing *The Organic Gardeners Handbook of Natural Pest and Disease Control* by: Fern Marshall Bradley, Barbara W. Ellis and Deborah L. Martin. You won't be disappointed with their contribution to this realm.

Chapter 7

THE LAST WORD: FINAL TIPS AND THOUGHTS

I think this is what hooks one to gardening: it is the closest one can come to being present at creation. ~ Phyllis Theroux

GENERAL MAINTENANCE

All gardens require basic maintenance. The primary focus of this book is to help you begin your garden, but here are a few additional tips that should guide you in the early stages.

Deadheading

My introduction to deadheading came via a short, round lady with a dollop of white hair like meringue atop her head. I'd planted a box of petunias and been enjoying their royal purple blossoms for a few weeks when I heard a knock on my door. As I opened the mahogany door of the century home where we were renting, she announced, "You need to start deadheading." Being an American and given my relative newness to Ontario, I immediately assumed this must be a Canadian expression I had yet to hear. In the end, I discovered that it wasn't an exclusively Canadian expression and that it would encourage my petunias to blossom.

Before You Begin

In a new garden, you may wish to leave some blossoms once they're spent. Why? Well, when the blossom is spent, seed pods develop. Nature's way of propagating itself, seed pods hold seeds that eventually become new plants. If I have an infant garden and desire more of a certain plant, I will sometimes leave the plant to do its own thing for a year or two. Rose campion spreads prolifically through reseeding. Those fuchsia petals become one inch deep pods holding thousands of tiny seeds. I often leave them to spread on their own; the following spring I'm rewarded with dozens of new velvety grey-green plants.

However, should you prefer to have more control over where the seeds go, or the number of pods you actually have, you may want to go ahead and deadhead most of the spent flowers of a plant leaving only a few chances for propagation. You may also wish to leave the spent flowers until the seedpods are all fully developed and then snip the seedpods, saving them to dry out for replanting somewhere else. The options are limitless, but don't be overwhelmed, in your early days of gardening, deadheading is not the most urgent need. However, since deadheading can encourage new flower production by allowing all the nutrients the plant is sending up to buds to go to new buds instead of the old, spent flower, it is time well used.

How to Deadhead

It's really not that complicated; I promise. Check your garden about once a week for spent flowers. When you notice blossoms drooping, laying over, petals falling etc., you'll want to pinch or snip them off your plant. Some people prefer garden sheers to pinching between their fingers, and indeed, in some cases like daylilies for example, a garden sheer is more precise and less likely to affect the other flower buds. I typically deadhead during my morning stroll through the garden with my favorite mug of steaming coffee in one hand and the thumb and pointer of my other hand poised to pinch spent blossoms.

Cutting Back

Many beautiful plants like tulips and daffodils are delightful during their bloom time, but leave much to be desired once their petals have fluttered to the ground. Still, their leaves have an important job to do. Until their leaves turn brown and die back, they provide needed nutrition to the bulbs. Remember that bulb plants make more bulbs which mean more blooms the following year. As a rule, I try to do two things with bulb plants: (1) Group them with other plants that flower immediately after they are spent and (2) Allow them to die back *before* trimming them. For example, by planting tulips with daffodils and daylilies, you will enjoy daffodils' bright yellow blooms followed by the lovely inverted bell-shape of tulips, then the vivid orange garden standby, the daylily. The bright flowers of the tulip will distract from the browning foliage of the daffodil.

Other plants such as Rudbeckia may reward you with more flowers if you give them a good haircut after their first showing of yellow blooms. Consult sources such as davesgarden.com or classygroundcovers.com for more information on how your perennials will respond to a mid-season trim.

Dividing

Over time, many perennials will outgrow their homes. That's when you get to add more flower beds or share some of your thriving flora with friends. Many people are intimidated by the task of dividing, but it is really very straightforward.

1. You will encounter varying opinions about the best time to divide your perennials. It can be done in early spring before blooming or early fall after blooming. My general rule of thumb is that I wait to divide my earliest flowering plants until they are done blooming. My phlox, for example, flowers in March where I live. I wait until it has finished flowering, and then divide it. It is still early enough in spring to be cut and set in a new home. However, plants

that flower more than a month after your last frost can be divided before they flower. You want the plant to have enough time to recover from the shock of being divided and still give you flowers that season.

2. Dig a large perimeter around the section of plant you wish to remove. (Some people prefer to dig the entire plant up so they can see the roots where they are dividing.) Be certain you have dug deeply enough to get to the bottom of your root system. (If you dig the entire plant up, you will be able to see if you have done so.)

3. With a swift motion, slice straight down through the plant at the point where you wish to divide it. (A straight shovel works best, but I have used a lawn edger or rounded shovel also.)

4. Return the portion of the plant you wish to keep to the ground. (I like to add a bit of well-aged compost to fill the hole.)

5. Give it a good drink and apologize for the shock.

6. Share or plant the other portion. If it will not be placed in the ground right away, make certain that it has a healthy soil in a good sized pot as well as a good drink of water.

Remember that dividing is not so much a science as common sense. Don't divide baby plants. Wait until they are hearty, well established and ready to be broken into smaller sections. If in doubt, consider what a baby version of your plant looks like at the garden center. If you think you can make a few plants that size from your large plant, go ahead and divide it. If you aren't certain, wait a year.

Weeding

I tend to be of Ralph Waldo Emerson's camp who said, "What is a weed? A weed is a plant whose virtues have not yet been discovered." Famous for letting it grow a little longer just to see what type of flower it will produce, weeding is not my favorite garden chore. The very thought of pulling out anything remotely green with roots goes against everything within me. Alas, though, weeding must be done. A few plants left to grow soon become an army of invaders, and the perennials you placed so carefully will experience a slow death by choking. You may feel ruthless yanking those little invaders, but I promise you, they grow quickly and will take over before you know what's happened.

My favorite time to pull weeds is after a soft, soaking rain. The soil gives up the intruders with ease, and as long as they've not gone to seed, I pile them in a basket to be added to my compost. Though not welcome in your garden, they are an excellent addition of nitrogen rich organic matter for your compost. (They will add nitrogen and other nutrients to my pile.) It may prove helpful to label your plants if you put them in as tender babies. This way when a weed (who will grow three times as fast) crops up right beside your plant, you'll know which is which. If you've worked hard to create a specific type of bed, don't fall victim to Emerson's thinking: Pull your weeds!

Last Words

Most people who have never attempted to garden will tell me they don't have a green thumb. Mine wasn't always green. Sometimes I think it still isn't green. At the time of writing this book, I have a large red clay bank void of plants glaring at me daily. We recently moved; our new home required some leveling of the back yard. When my brother-in-law and husband were done creating their football-field lawn, I was left with a bank I hadn't counted on planting.

I stared at that space for a few weeks before I began to visualize what might be a game-plan suitable for it. One side will have a large section of blueberries--some from a local garden center and others from a dear friend in her seventies whose blueberries are famous around here. Behind the blueberries, I've placed a row of forsythia as a hedge dividing the wooded area behind from the garden and lawn. Beneath them, I've added lavender phlox to cover the ground over time. I don't know if the phlox will work out or not. It's an experiment of sorts. The soil is right for it, but I don't know how it will work under blueberry plants. I'll need to add a walkway/steps in order to pick the blueberries without disturbing the phlox.

Sometimes gardens are like that. You try things, and if they work out, great. If not, that's alright too. The truth is, our thumbs are as green as we make them. Like everything else in life, practice indeed makes perfect. In the case of gardening, the first step to green thumbs is just that: taking the first step. Choose a garden spot, amend your soil, select plants, put them in, care for them with love, and most likely, when you look down, you'll notice the tips of your thumbs turning the shade of your garden's foliage. More importantly, you will have contributed to the environment, gained a lifetime hobby, and added to the beauty of creation. How can you possibly go wrong? Get out there and garden!

References

"All-Purpose Insect Pest Spray." *Organic Gardening.*
Rodale Inc., n.d. Web. 22 Apr 2013.
<http://www.organicgardening.com/learn-and-grow/all-purpose-insect-pest-spray>.

"Analyzing, Improving and Amending Your Soil."
www.garden-soil.com. N.p., n.d. Web. 22 Apr 2013.
<http://www.garden-soil.com/garden-soil-fertilizers-10.html>.

"Average First and Last Frost Dates by State." *Victory Seeds.* N.p.. Web. 22 Apr 2013.
<http://www.victoryseeds.com/frost/>.

Bartholomew, Mel. *The All New Square Foot Gardening.*
Nashville: Cool Springs Press, 2006. Print.

Bradley, F.M., B.W. Ellis, and . *The Organic Gardener's Handbook of Natural Pest and Disease Control: A Complete Guide To Maintaining a Healthy Garden and Yard the Earth-Friendly Way.* New York, NY: Rodale, 2009. Print.

"Buy Mail Order Plants, Seeds, & Bulbs - PlantScout - Dave's Garden." *Dave's Garden*. N.p.. Web. 22 Apr 2013. <http://davesgarden.com/products/ps/>.

"Cooperative Extensions." *ClassyGroundcovers*. N.p.. Web. 22 Apr 2013. <http://classygroundcovers.com/site/page?view=cooperativeextensions>.

Easy to Grow Bulbs for Warm Weather Gardens. N.p.. Web. 22 Apr 2013. <http://www.easytogrowbulbs.com/>.

"Garden 'Mini' Insectary." *eartheasy Solutions For Sustainable Living*. N.p.. Web. 22 Apr 2013. <http://eartheasy.com/grow_garden_insectary.htm>.

"Garden Watchdog." *Dave's Garden*. N.p.. Web. 22 Apr 2013. <http://davesgarden.com/products/gwd/>.

"How to Plant." *ClassyGroundcovers*. N.p.. Web. 22 Apr 2013. <http://classygroundcovers.com/site/page?view=BareRootTutorial>.

Hulme, Fred. "Nutrition Myths That Can Damage Your Crops." *everris.us.com*. GMPro, n.d. Web. 22 Apr

2013. <http://everris.us.com/nutrition-myths-can-damage-your-crops>.

"List of Repellent Plants." *Wikipedia the Free Encyclopedia*. N.p.. Web. 22 Apr 2013. <http://en.wikipedia.org/wiki/List_of_repellent_plants>.

Mazzoni, Mary. "The Benefits of Using Compost in Your Garden." *www.earth911.com*. N.p., 13 Mar 2013. Web. 22 Apr 2013. <http://earth911.com/news/2007/04/02/benefits-of-using-compost/>.

"Natural Garden Pest Control." *eartheasy Solutions For Sustainable Living*. N.p., 2012. Web. 22 Apr 2013. <http://eartheasy.com/grow_nat_pest_cntrl.htm>.

"Nearly Half of All American Homeowners Give a Green Thumbs-Up to Home Improvements." *Scarborough Research*. N.p., 07 May 2012. Web. 22 Apr 2013. <http://www.scarborough.com/press_releases/Scarborough-Gardening-Homeowners-Market-Research.pdf>.

Onalee's Seeds, LLC. N.p.. Web. 22 Apr 2013. <http://www.onaleeseeds.com/>.

Organic Pest Control Techniques." *Organic Gardening.*
Rodale Inc., n.d. Web. 22 Apr 2013. <
http://www.organicgardening.com/learn-and-
grow/organic-pest-control-techniques>.

"P. Allen Smith Garden Home." *Pest Control Plants.* N.p..
Web. 22 Apr 2013.
<http://www.pallensmith.com/articles/pest-control-
plants>.

Page, Russel. *The Education of a Gardener.* London:
Harvill, 1995. Print.

Phillips, S. *The Practical Gardening Encyclopedia.* 4th.
Burnaby: Select Publications, 2004. Print.

"Plant Calculator." *ClassyGroundcovers.* N.p.. Web. 22
Apr 2013.
<http://classygroundcovers.com/site/page?view=plant
Calculator>.

"PlantFiles: The Largest Plant Identification Reference
Guide - Dave's Garden." *Dave's Garden.* N.p.. Web.
22 Apr 2013. <http://davesgarden.com/guides/pf/>.

Rain Bird. N.p.. Web. 22 Apr 2013.
<http://www.rainbird.com/>.

"Soil Basics." *www.gardening.cornell.edu.* N.p.. Web. 22
    Apr 2013.
    <http://www.gardening.cornell.edu/factsheets/misc/so
    ilbasics.html>.

"Talking Trees An Urban Forestry Toolkit for Local
    Governments." *milliontreesnyc.* N.p., n.d. Web. 22
    Apr 2013.
    <http://www.milliontreesnyc.org/downloads/pdf/talki
    ng_trees_urban_forestry_toolkit.pdf>.

"Tropaeolum majus." *Wikipedia the Free Encyclopedia.*
    N.p., 07 Mar 2013. Web. 22 Apr 2013.
    <http://en.wikipedia.org/wiki/Tropaeolum_majus>.

Vanderlinden, Colleen. "15 Homemade Organic Gardening
    Sprays and Concoctions That Actually Work." *TLC.*
    Planet Green. Web. 22 Apr 2013.

19961754R10059

Made in the USA
Charleston, SC
20 June 2013